Union Public Library

HIP-HOP

One word can be used to describe hip-hop powerhouse OutKast— unique. Whether talking about their fashion or their music, Big Boi and André 3000 go their own direction.

Hip-Hop

OutKast

Jacquelyn Simone

Union Public Library

Mason Crest Publishers

OutKast

Copyright © 2008 by Mason Crest Publishers. All rights reserved. No part of this publication may be reproduced or transmitted in any form or by any means, electronic or mechanical, including photocopying, recording, taping, or any information storage and retrieval system, without permission from the publisher.

Produced by Harding House Publishing Service, Inc.
201 Harding Avenue, Vestal, NY 13850.

MASON CREST PUBLISHERS INC.
370 Reed Road
Broomall, Pennsylvania 19008
(866)MCP-BOOK (toll free)
www.masoncrest.com

Printed in the United States of America

First Printing

9 8 7 6 5 4 3 2 1

Library of Congress Cataloging-in-Publication Data

Simone, Jacquelyn.
  OutKast / Jacquelyn Simone.
     p. cm. — (Hip-hop)
  Includes index.
  ISBN 978-1-4222-0301-9
  ISBN: 978-1-4222-0077-3 (series)
 1. OutKast (Musical group)—Juvenile literature. 2. Rap musicians—United States—Biography—Juvenile literature. I. Title.
ML3930.O9S56 2008
782.421649092'2—dc22
[B]
                                        2007032958

Publisher's notes:
• All quotations in this book come from original sources and contain the spelling and grammatical inconsistencies of the original text.

• The Web sites mentioned in this book were active at the time of publication. The publisher is not responsible for Web sites that have changed their addresses or discontinued operation since the date of publication. The publisher will review and update the Web site addresses each time the book is reprinted.

DISCLAIMER: The following story has been thoroughly researched, and to the best of our knowledge, represents a true story. While every possible effort has been made to ensure accuracy, the publisher will not assume liability for damages caused by inaccuracies in the data, and makes no warranty on the accuracy of the information contained herein. This story has not been authorized nor endorsed by OutKast.

Contents

Hip-Hop Time Line

1970s DJ Kool Herc pioneers the use of breaks, isolations, and repeats using two turn-tables.

1976 Grandmaster Flash and the Furious Five emerge as one of the first battlers and freestylers.

1984 The track "Roxanne Roxanne" sparks the first diss war.

1982 Afrika Bambaataa tours Europe in another hip-hop first.

1988 Hip-hop record sales reach 100 million annually.

1970s Grafitti artist Vic begins tagging on New York subways.

1980 Rapper Kurtis Blow sells a million records and makes the first nationwide TV appearance for a hip-hop artist.

1985 The film *Krush Groove*, about the rise of Def Jam Records, is released.

1970 1980

1970s The central elements of the hip-hop culture begin to emerge in the Bronx, New York City.

1983 Ice-T releases his first singles, marking the earliest examples of gangsta rap.

1986 Run DMC cover Aerosmith's "Walk this Way" and appear on the cover of *Rolling Stone*.

1979 "Rapper's Delight," by The Sugarhill Gang, goes gold.

1974 Afrika Bambaataa organizes the Universal Zulu Nation.

1984 *Graffitti Rock*, the first hip-hop television program, premieres.

1981 Grandmaster Flash and the Furious Five release *Adventures on the Wheels of Steel*.

1988 MTV premieres *Yo! MTV Raps*.

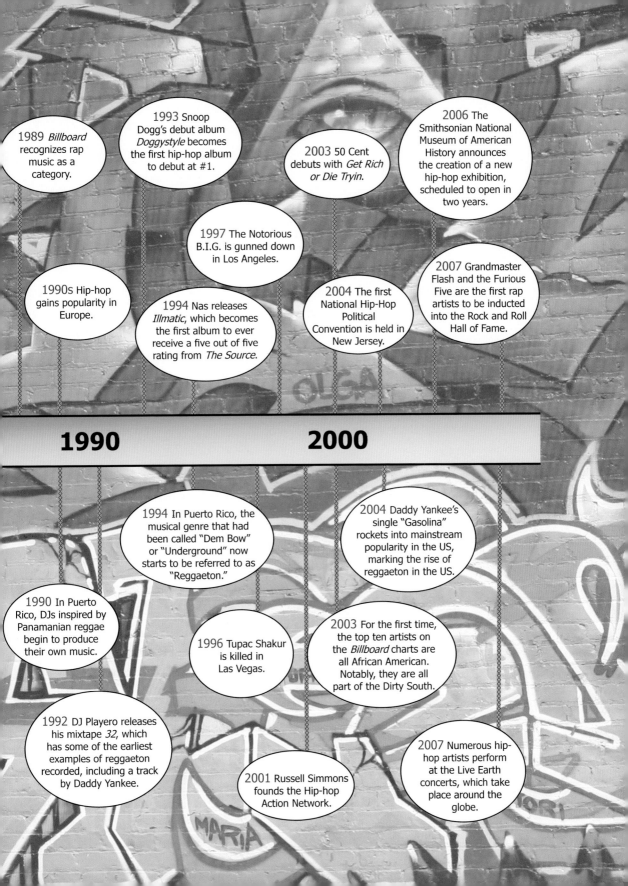

1989 *Billboard* recognizes rap music as a category.

1993 Snoop Dogg's debut album *Doggystyle* becomes the first hip-hop album to debut at #1.

2003 50 Cent debuts with *Get Rich or Die Tryin.*

2006 The Smithsonian National Museum of American History announces the creation of a new hip-hop exhibition, scheduled to open in two years.

1997 The Notorious B.I.G. is gunned down in Los Angeles.

1990s Hip-hop gains popularity in Europe.

2007 Grandmaster Flash and the Furious Five are the first rap artists to be inducted into the Rock and Roll Hall of Fame.

1994 Nas releases *Illmatic*, which becomes the first album to ever receive a five out of five rating from *The Source*.

2004 The first National Hip-Hop Political Convention is held in New Jersey.

1990

2000

1994 In Puerto Rico, the musical genre that had been called "Dem Bow" or "Underground" now starts to be referred to as "Reggaeton."

2004 Daddy Yankee's single "Gasolina" rockets into mainstream popularity in the US, marking the rise of reggaeton in the US.

1990 In Puerto Rico, DJs inspired by Panamanian reggae begin to produce their own music.

1996 Tupac Shakur is killed in Las Vegas.

2003 For the first time, the top ten artists on the *Billboard* charts are all African American. Notably, they are all part of the Dirty South.

1992 DJ Playero releases his mixtape *32*, which has some of the earliest examples of reggaeton recorded, including a track by Daddy Yankee.

2001 Russell Simmons founds the Hip-hop Action Network.

2007 Numerous hip-hop artists perform at the Live Earth concerts, which take place around the globe.

Generally, uniqueness is a good thing. It certainly has been for Big Boi (left) and André 3000 (right). Their music has brought them many fans and many awards. They certainly stand out from others in hip-hop.

OutKasts in the In Crowd

The flashing cameras seemed dull compared to their broad smiles. On February 27, 2002, the crowd outside the Staples Center in Los Angeles yelled to the two men, begging for a picture or autograph. The duo was not only set apart from the other celebrities by their noticeable star power, but also by their interesting fashion choices.

The taller of the men wore a pastel yellow and blue plaid outfit, and he was probably the only person on the red carpet wearing knickers that day. The second man was shorter, and he was more serious as he watched the crowd. He wore a baby-blue suit. Both men wore large white hats, which made the pair stand out from the crowd of photographers and celebrities. Even without the unique outfits, however, the crowd would have recognized them as one of the most original and popular rap groups on the modern music scene. The 44th Annual Grammy Awards proved what the world had known for a while: OutKast was a group to watch.

As the awards ceremony proceeded, the members of the rap duo, André 3000 and Big Boi, abandoned their stylish clothes for more bizarre outfits. André donned a flared pink jumpsuit, which was made even more startling by a platinum blonde wig beneath a fuzzy black hat. Big Boi chose a slightly more conventional costume: he wore a black hat and a green suit. Once the audience recovered from the initial shock caused by the costumes, they were treated to an energetic performance of the OutKast hit "Ms. Jackson." The duo rapped and sang while lights flashed, children break-danced, and people with tambourines walked through the aisles and onto the stage. Many critics and viewers praised it as the best performance of the evening.

The song was not the only success for OutKast at the Grammy's that night. Although OutKast had received another nomination three years earlier, the 2002 award ceremony, which acknowledged work released the previous year, brought them their first two trophies at what is considered the most notable awards ceremony in the music industry. OutKast received honors for Best Rap Performance by a Duo or Group for "Ms. Jackson" and Best Rap Album for *Stankonia*. Their Best Rap Album Award was made even more impressive by the talent of their competitors: they beat Eve, Ja Rule, Jay-Z, and Ludacris. Their other nominations were the prestigious Album of the Year for *Stankonia*, Record of the Year for "Ms. Jackson," and Best Short Form Music Video for "Ms. Jackson." Although they didn't win in these categories, simply being considered for the awards is a tremendous compliment. These honors made it clear that OutKast was a major force in the music world. In any case, many would claim that OutKast won the unofficial awards for the most unique outfits and best live performance during the show. Years later, they have upheld their reputation for musical excellence and continue to question the norms of the *mainstream*.

What's That Sound?

Their popularity is a little ironic when you consider the meaning of the group's name: OutKast is the dictionary pronunciation script for the word "outcast," which means homeless or not accepted in society. In light of the group's broad influence and record sales, it is hard to argue that society does not accept them. Instead, the group's name most likely means that the duo's sound breaks away from the mainstream; they

So how does one define OutKast's music? No one knows for sure, not even Big Boi and André 3000. They take a little bit from one genre, some from another, and more from elsewhere. Somehow, they have the skill to put all the parts together to create a cohesive tapestry of sounds.

Being a star is all about glitz and glam, right? Well, maybe for some musicians, but not OutKast. Or perhaps their definition of glitz and glam is different from that of other big-name performers.

are creative outcasts. When they first appeared on the music scene, listeners and industry experts alike were startled by how unique they sounded. OutKast's style, lyrics, delivery, and entire package were unlike anything most hip-hop fans had ever heard. L.A. Reid, the head of OutKast's LaFace label, told Rolling Stone that the famous musician Prince praised André as an artist "so against the grain in terms of what's happening on the radio."

Appropriately, one of their albums was titled *ATLiens*; their sound seems to come from another musical universe. Although each OutKast songs are unique, most share certain elements. The traditional OutKast song includes Big Boi and André 3000 alternating rapping verses, and there is usually a catchy, sung chorus. This pattern highlights the difference between the two artists' rap styles. Big Boi delivers the lyrics in a fast, deep voice, while André includes higher interjections and melodies during his own verses. André's verses are seen as introspective and observational, meaning that they have deep and thoughtful messages about the world and himself, while Big Boi's style is more confrontational and in your face. Whoever is rapping, the lyrics always include creative rhymes and an interesting view of life.

OutKast's **genre** is nearly impossible to define, because they combine elements of **funk**, jazz, and rock in their hip-hop songs. Music critics have struggled to find a single category into which OutKast falls, and they have made complicated descriptions in an effort to discuss the pair's creative style. Chris Campion of London's Observer, for example, called André "a lanky beatnik given to talking like a lovelorn dandy from a Jane Austen novel." Such a description does not fit the average rap artist!

Not even OutKast can define its music easily. "The beauty of OutKast is people can't pin us to one category," Big Boi explained to VH1 in 2003.

"You got to expect the unexpected. Whatever the vibe flowing through my brain to Dré's brain and back is never gonna be the same thing. We never try to imitate what we've done in the past. We stay in our own little world tucked away. We're still listening to what's going on, but it just comes out like that. We're just OutKast, apart from the norm. That's what we stand for."

André 3000 and Big Boi have called their work "slumadelic," which means that their lyrics have positive messages about the real stories of American life. Instead of filling their songs with violence and drug references, as is common in hip-hop music, OutKast has covered many different subjects, from the state of the modern family and relationships to the civil rights movement to dancing. In all areas of their music and image, the duo is certainly unique!

Hip-Hop History

Even though their sound is unique, the musical genre into which OutKast most clearly falls is hip-hop. This style of music was formed in the United States in the mid-1970s and became a significant part of modern pop **culture** by the following decade. The two main elements of hip-hop are rapping (also known as MCing) and production and **scratching** (DJing). Hip-hop culture is made up of these, along with hip-hop dancing and urban art such as graffiti. The cultural craze of hip-hop in the United States can be traced back to the African American and Latino communities of the Bronx, a New York City borough.

In the early 1970s, DJs began taking out the percussion break (or beat portion) from funk and disco songs and creating a new sound by combining and layering the sound samples. MCs were responsible for introducing DJs and keeping the audience excited. MCs started to speak more between songs, urging people to dance, and their words gradually became more stylized and rhythmic. As they began to speak over the DJ's track, a radical new music style called rapping emerged.

Modern DJs typically use two turntables, a mixer, an amplifier, speakers, and other basic equipment to create the desired sound. MCs often attempt to out-rap each other in intense "battles." Beat boxing is also increasing in popularity after fading from popular culture for years. This involves creating beats that sound like drums and basses using only the human voice.

Hip-hop remains popular even though it has been criticized for encouraging drug use, profanities, and misogyny (the hatred of women). The culture that came from this musical genre has had a major impact on modern fashion, language, and other parts of society in the United States and overseas.

Hip-hop music is characterized by rhythmic lyrics that often use assonance (the repetition of vowel sounds), alliteration (the repetition of initial sounds), and rhyme. The rapper is accompanied by a beat that can be created by a DJ, producer, and instrumentalists. Other sampled, synthesized, or performed sounds can also appear on the track.

By the early twenty-first century, hip-hop had become one of the best-selling music genres in the world. At the same time, OutKast was emerging as one of the most successful rap groups on the music scene. The popularity of hip-hop music in mainstream culture catapulted OutKast to fame—and the group's innovative style will undoubtedly keep it in the spotlight for years to come.

Just because hip-hop was born in New York City, that doesn't mean all of the genre's big names came from there. Atlanta, Georgia—ATL—is the home of many stars, including Big Boi and André 3000.

The ATL Years

Life was not always full of red carpets and *platinum*-selling albums for André 3000 or Big Boi. In fact, both had difficult family situations and had to rise above many struggles to achieve success in the music industry. Even though they left behind their childhoods and traded in poverty for millions of dollars, they never forgot where they came from. The years they spent in Atlanta, Georgia, which they lovingly refer to as ATL, left a permanent mark on their personalities, their lives, and their music.

When Big Boi Was Little

On the day Antwan André Patton was born, February 1, 1975, in Savannah, Georgia, his parents had no idea he would one day sell millions of records under the name Big Boi. His mother, Rowena Patton, was only fifteen years old when he was born. Since his father, Tony Kearse, was just eighteen and soon joined the Marines,

Rowena turned to her relatives to help support herself and the baby. The young family lived with several extended family members in a three-bedroom colonial house in Savannah. The rooms were cramped, but a crowded home was better than none at all.

Antwan later had four younger siblings, which made it more difficult for his mother to support the family. Their extended family saved them from poverty, but they were still not rich by any means. As a result, Antwan learned the value of a dollar, and from a young age, he was hatching schemes to make money. As a child, he would invite other children over to his house and charge them a cover fee, meaning that they had to pay to come in. His mischievous nature eventually led him down a dark path: when his family moved from Savannah to Atlanta, he ran the city streets and began to spend his time with the wrong crowd.

In spite of the temptation of urban gangs and violence, Antwan was still an intelligent, kind person. His friends came from all races and *ethnicities*, and he never discriminated against people because they were not African American like he was. His sense of humor and talents made him well liked by other students.

Not only was he an athletic star on the football field and in other sports at Tri-Cities High School for the Performing Arts, but he also displayed gifts in music and academics. He showed a gift for writing lyrics from a young age: his family recalls that he always carried a pen and paper with him to write down any rhymes that came to his mind during the day. He was fascinated by all music genres, not just hip-hop, and he listened to music constantly. Although he did not know what the future would bring, Antwan's musical talents would one day make him famous.

Surprisingly, however, Antwan did not imagine a future career in music for himself. As he told *People*, he wanted to either be a child psychologist or play football. He had plenty of experience with children due to his large family and popularity, and his impressive high school football career made an athletic career a possibility. His grades were high enough that he could have easily received a scholarship to a good university, where he could have prepared for either of those fields. Antwan realized the importance of an education and graduated from high school with an impressive 3.68 grade point average. This means that he was almost a straight-A student.

A Quiet Kid Named André

The man who would later make hits with Antwan under the stage name André 3000 was born on May 27, 1975. Long before he became one-half of OutKast, he was called André Lauren Benjamin. His mother, Sharon Benjamin, was also young when she had her only child, and she took care of him on her own.

Even as a baby, André displayed an interest in music. "The things that babies play with, he wouldn't play with," his mother told VH1.

> *"You would just put him on the blanket, give him some newspaper and he'll just take the paper and he'll just crumble it. . . . He loved the sound."*

Since he did not have any siblings, he did not talk much. André has said that a lot of attention and crowds still make him uncomfortable because his childhood was somewhat lonely.

Sharon and André were poor, and they frequently had to move from one home to another in southwest Atlanta because they did not have enough money to pay the rent. Sharon remembers that André seemed to understand his mother's situation, even when he was very young. "I would tell him," she said to VH1, "'Dré, let's go.' 'I'm ready, Mama,' he'd say." He and his mother always carried on.

Despite their poverty, Sharon insisted that André would have a successful life. As she told VH1's *Driven*, she "raised him to be clean-cut and preppy." She saw a quality education as the key to helping her son break out of the ghetto, and she was determined to give him every opportunity other children had. Through Atlanta's Minority to Majority program, which tried to help African Americans and other minority children go to good schools, Sharon had André take a bus to a mostly white, wealthy school to pursue his artistic interests. André went to Tri-Cities School for the Performing Arts in the Atlanta suburb of East Point.

This exposure to rich kids made André realize he could one day rise to their level. He exercised his creativity in his efforts to fit in with the other students. André also developed an interest in upper-middle-class fashions in his early teens, but he could not afford the designer brands, like Ralph Lauren, that the other students wore. Instead of complaining to his mother, he fastened his own self-designed logo onto plain white shirts. In this way, the man who would eventually be known for his unique fashion sense began creating his own outfits.

Even though he had these educational and creative opportunities, André's personal life was rocky. When he was sixteen years old, he rebelled against his mother and let his grades drop. He turned to a negative urban lifestyle as a means of survival. As a result, Sharon sent him to live with his father, Lawrence Walker. Lawrence was a collections agent, and Sharon hoped he would be a good role model for their son. Instead, André saw his father as more of a friend than an authority figure, and he got into even more trouble. The teenager skipped school to go to clubs and parties, and he dropped out of school completely during his junior year. He later earned his high school equivalency, but his mother was hurt by his lack of appreciation for the sacrifices she had made to get him into a high-quality school. After all, despite all of his mother's efforts, André Benjamin's future looked gloomy.

Music Brought Them Together

When their paths came together, the fates of Antwan Patton and André Benjamin were changed forever. Since they both attended Tri-Cities High School, which was an arts-magnet school in East Point, Atlanta, the teachers and administrators encouraged students to express themselves. It was common for students to compete against each other in rap battles and other activities during lunch or after school. It was through

André 3000 has had a love of fashion since his childhood. He couldn't afford clothing like his classmates wore, but he could develop his own style. In this photo, André 3000 poses with Ghostface Killah (left) of the Wu-Tang Clan. Could they be sharing fashion tips?

these battles that Antwan and André met during their sophomore year. They quickly became *freestyle*-rhyme rivals, and their competition developed into a deeper appreciation for each other's techniques and abilities. Both young men had "street cred," meaning that their difficult lives and involvement in urban activities made their gritty raps more believable. Neither one had an easy life, but they were both gifted enough to attend a performing arts high school. Although Antwan and André had different personalities and experiences, they soon found that they understood each other very well. That bond would continue throughout the years and help them as they earned fame. "We go through our times where we might

Tri-Cities School for the Performing Arts, located in East Point, Georgia, brought together the duo that would one day become OutKast. They were encouraged to develop their artistic talents. The future André 3000 and Big Boi met during one of the rap battles, which were popular after-school activities.

not see eye to eye but we always compromise," Big Boi commented to VH1.

"You got to be able to come to some point where everybody agrees and move forward. Me and Dré have always been able to do that, 'cause we started out as best friends before we started doing music."

Their shared interest in rap strengthened their friendship, and they decided to make music with each other instead of competing against each other. The two teens hung out at East Point parking lots and malls, where they performed under the name 2 Shades Deep. Their rapping nicknames were Black Dog and Black Wolf. And they continued rapping together even after André dropped out of Tri-Cities High School. Before long, they would rise from rapping for crowds at parking lots to impressing millions of fans on stage.

A Broad Range of Influences

As the duo began to form their unique sound, the influence of other musicians became more obvious in their music. Throughout their lives, both Antwan and André appreciated various genres of music. They were inspired by and borrowed different elements of the music they loved. Antwan listened to Run D.M.C., Parliament, and funk pioneer George Clinton. He remembers watching concerts at Grant Park in Atlanta, and he learned performance styles from artists such as the Ohio Players. Meanwhile, since André went to mainly white schools, he developed an interest in different music. He listened to "white" music such as ZZ Top, Sting, Madonna, and the Smiths. He was also introduced to some **R&B**, soul, and rap artists, as he listened to Prince, the Funkadelic, John Coltrane, and 2 Live Crew. The wide range of both Antwan and André's musical influences shaped their later success. They would eventually sell millions of records as a stylistically **diverse** duo.

The group that became OutKast was not an overnight success. But they worked hard, kept at it, went through a name change, and built up their self-confidence as performers. The result? Hit records, awards, and passionately loyal fans.

The Innovators Invade

Antwan and André delivered smooth rhymes with impressive skill, and 2 Shades Deep was quickly gaining a local fan base. Rapping was only a hobby for them, but one that would eventually lead to their stardom.

Their big break came when they met with Atlanta's Organized Noize Production trio. The production group had been responsible for such successful acts as TLC, En Vogue, and Goodie Mob. A girlfriend introduced Antwan and André to Rico Wade, one of the well-known Organized Noize producers. Wade agreed to hear 2 Shades Deep perform in the parking lot of an East Point store. The producer was so impressed that he immediately drove the duo to his studio.

The Organized Noize studio was called the Dungeon, because it was an unfinished red clay basement. Antwan and André were thrilled to be discovered by such a talented producer, and they spent as much time as they possibly could in the Dungeon. Other rising Atlanta music artists also went to the Dungeon on a regular basis, so 2 Shades Deep was inspired by the creativity of their peers. The artists of the Dungeon became like a family, and OutKast still mentions them during some songs. In this setting, surrounded by other people with a passion for music, Antwan and André went from being two teenagers who rapped for fun to two determined aspiring artists.

Rejection and Success

Now that they were under the guidance of Organized Noize, 2 Shades Deep began to look for a record label. Wade arranged an audition, and Antwan and André soon performed for Antonio "L.A." Reid. This was an important audition, because Reid was the cofounder, with Kenneth "Babyface" Edmonds, of LaFace Records, an imprint of Arista Records. The young duo realized that this one performance could determine the direction of their careers, and their nerves prevented them from doing their best. Reid rejected them after the audition because he thought they lacked star quality.

Despite this early setback, Antwan and André refused to give up. They returned to the Dungeon, where Organized Noize helped them improve their lyrics and delivery. Wade knew from the first time he saw them rap in a parking lot that 2 Shades Deep could become one of the most unique groups in the music industry. They had the raw talent; all they needed was confidence and a little pizzazz.

Bouncing back from their rejection, Antwan and André auditioned again. This time Reid was impressed by the teenage duo because of the skills they had developed with Organized Noize. He recognized in the group the same quality that had caught Wade's attention: individuality. They were unlike the other popular rappers at the time, and their refusal to follow the mainstream would make them famous.

Reid offered them a contract, but they were only seventeen at the time and their parents wanted them to wait another year. Since they needed their parents to cosign the contract, they had no choice but to wait. Reid's offer was significant because they were the first rap group signed to the label, which focused mainly on R&B artists. When the day finally came to sign the contract, the eighteen-year-olds were overjoyed. "We just wanted a shot and L.A. Reid gave us that shot," Big Boi told VH1.

> *"It wasn't even so much about getting paid, because I think the advance was like 15 grand. We were kids, so to us, that was great. That was gonna set us straight for a minute and give us a chance to go in the studio. We didn't have to work our regular jobs anymore."*

In fact, their future jobs would be anything but "regular"!

 Having a Ball

With their achievement, came some changes. First, they replaced the name 2 Shades Deep with "OutKast." The duo was flipping through a dictionary and thought that "outcast" suited them since East Coast and West Coast rappers dominated the hip-hop industry at that time, and Southerners were considered outsiders. Also, Antwan changed his performing name to "Big Boi," which was ironic because he's short. André went by the simple name of Dré.

The newly named duo then set to work. As their first act with LaFace, they appeared on a **remix** of TLC's "What About Your Friends." L.A. Reid then invited OutKast to make a song for a Christmas album. The result was "Player's Ball," a heartfelt rap that complains about the lack of cheer in the ghetto. Since both Antwan and André had struggled with poverty and had run the streets of Atlanta, the message was close to their hearts. Live instrumentation gave the song a funky style.

Audiences were instantly attracted to OutKast's socially conscious lyrics and smooth delivery. "Player's Ball" rose to #1 on the *Billboard* rap charts and held the top position for an impressive six weeks. It was eventually certified gold by the

Recording Industry Association of America (RIAA), meaning that it sold at least 500,000 copies. Across the country, radios were already playing OutKast's music.

Long Name, Big Fame

With a hit single to their credit, OutKast needed to develop a debut album. They wanted to represent their Southern roots and offer a unique contribution to the music industry. "We came in hungry and busting and never relaxed," Big Boi re-

When "Player's Ball" hit #1, people all over the country started to pay attention to Big Boi (shown in this photo) and André 3000. Interviewers wanted to talk to them, and people actually seemed to care about what they had to say.

called to VH1. "Stay on top of your game, and it will go where it's gonna go."

Under the production expertise of Organized Noize, Dré and Big Boi started writing lyrics and choosing beats. The result was *Southernplayalisticadillacmuzik*, an energetic full-length album that blended hip-hop, Southern guitar riffs, bubbling funk, and laidback '70s-style soul music. Notable tracks on the album included the title track and "Git Up, Git Out," which was a politically charged **collaboration** with Goodie Mob. The lyrics discussed the lifestyles of pimps and gangsters as well as the status of African Americans in the South. Such themes were more serious than most hip-hop artists' subject matter.

While they were recording *Southernplayalisticadillacmuzik*, André decided to permanently give up drinking, smoking, and consuming meat and dairy products. Big Boi was still a partier, and the contrast between the two helped attract a national fan base. André also began to dress eccentrically around this time. Although his bizarre fashion sense has been a main element of André's fame, at first it led to false rumors about his sexual orientation and mental health. People who choose to be different and express themselves in unique ways are often misunderstood, but André did not let the harsh gossip bring him down.

The highly anticipated album was released on April 26, 1994. Listeners loved the fresh sound, and the album soon hit the top 20. By the end of the year, the RIAA had certified the album platinum, which means that it sold over one million copies. OutKast received both popular and critical success; they were named Best New Rap Group of the Year at the 1995 Source Awards. The boys from the ATL were off to a strong start.

ATLiens

While enjoying their new success and critical praise, OutKast was also working on their next album. Since their confidence in their musical decisions was increasing as their celebrity status grew, they wanted to take more control in the creative process of their sophomore effort. OutKast partnered with David "Mr. DJ" Sheats and formed the Earthtone III production company. This partnership helped them produce some of their own **tracks**. For the most part, however, OutKast stuck with the formula that had propelled them to stardom and had Organized Noize produce the majority of the tracks.

ATLiens, which refers to their hometown of Atlanta as well as their extraterrestrial sound, was released on August 27, 1996. It featured futuristic beats and trance-like rhythms, which set OutKast apart from the mainstream even more than their debut album had. *ATLiens* reached the #2 position on the *Billboard* 200, and the title track was a top-40 hit. The song "*ATLiens*" discussed Dré's increasingly sober lifestyle as he raps, "No drugs or alcohol/so I can get the signal clear." The main hit from the album was "Elevators (Me and You)," which was certified gold and reached the #1 rap spot and the #12 place on the pop charts. The nation waited to hear what OutKast would come up with next.

Aquemini

The praise kept rolling in. September 29, 1998, brought the release of *Aquemini*, OutKast's most visionary project yet. Like *ATLiens*, the album reached the #2 spot on the *Billboard* 200. However, its reviews and record sales surpassed its predecessors: it was certified double platinum, meaning that it sold over two million copies. OutKast produced nine out of the fourteen tracks on *Aquemini*, which proved to the industry that they were even more talented than people had first thought. Critics praised the progressive vision of the album,

Being different can be hard. And when you're different and famous, well, that means there are more people who can criticize you or spread rumors. That's something André 3000 learned firsthand.

and the hip-hop publication *Source* gave it a perfect rating of "5 (out of 5) Mics."

It was no surprise that the album impressed and fascinated the masses. It infused jazz, reggae, and world beats, with collaborators such as Raekwon, funk pioneer George Clinton, and Goodie Mob. The lyrics were more spiritual and thoughtful than they had previously been, and there was a perfect balance between the heavy music on the first album and the heavy lyrical content of the sophomore album. The title was

Once OutKast released an album, its popularity grew even more. With each album, the duo's fame increased. *Aquemini* went multiplatinum, earning them superstar status. The album also showcased the pair's talents as producers.

fitting considering the tightness of the album as a whole. "*Aquemini* is the meeting of two worlds: the world of Aquarius & Gemini," explained Dré. "It's simply that two people can come together as one and create." Since Big Boi's zodiac sign is Aquarius and Dré's is Gemini, the title expressed that the two artists had merged into one being.

Despite this melding, they still maintained their contrasting personalities and musical styles, which helped create such an interesting blend. "I'm more street, hard-core hip-hop, and Dré's more extraterrestrial," Big Boi said. "Dré looks like the music and I look like the message." That combination proved to be magic as millions of fans gathered at record stores and concerts.

Legal Troubles

Unfortunately, the success of their third album was spoiled when civil rights pioneer Rosa Parks filed a lawsuit against OutKast and their label in 1999. The lead single on *Aquemini* was titled "Rosa Parks," but Rosa claimed that OutKast had unlawfully used her name to promote their music. Parks objected to some of the song's language, and she refused to have her name connected with it. She claimed that OutKast had violated her publicity and trademark rights.

Parks earned fame when she was arrested for refusing to move to the back of a public bus in Montgomery, Alabama, so that a white man could take her seat in 1955. Her actions started a boycott of the bus system by African Americans, and eventually led to court rulings that desegregated public transportation nationwide, so that people with any skin color could sit anywhere on buses.

Actually, OutKast's chorus was the only part that clearly hinted at Parks with the words, "Ah ha, hush that fuss/Everybody move to the back of the bus." OutKast explained that the chorus was to suggest that, just as Parks challenged the

In 1955, Rosa Parks took a stand by staying seated. Her arrest after she refused to give up her bus seat to a white man gave birth to the Montgomery bus boycott, a major event in civil rights history. The city's leaders thought the boycott would last only until the first rain. It lasted for more than a year.

norm of racial inequality, the rappers were eliminating hip-hop's old order. In a 1999 statement, the duo said,

> *"Rosa Parks has inspired our music and our lives since we were children. The opportunity to use our music to help educate young people about the heroes in the African-American community is one of the responsibilities we have as music artists."*

A court recognized that the rappers' intent was harmless and dismissed the case later that year.

However, in 2003, a three-judge panel in Ohio brought back part of the lawsuit. Parks said that she wanted all references to her removed from future versions of the record. OutKast responded that the First Amendment protected their freedom of speech and that the song was neither false advertising nor a violation of Parks' publicity rights. Parks' attorneys and caretaker re-filed the suit in 2004, and they asked for five billion dollars in damages. The suit was finally settled on April 15, 2005, with OutKast, their producers, and record labels paying a cash settlement and agreeing to work with the Rosa and Raymond Parks Institute for Self-Development to create educational programs about Rosa's life.

After years of lawsuits, OutKast and their labels still did not admit that they had done anything wrong. Ironically, in February 1999, the single "Rosa Parks" earned OutKast their first Grammy nomination for Best Rap Performance by a Duo or Group. The lawsuit was one blemish in an otherwise stellar career. But OutKast didn't let it slow them down.

Ever the fashion trendsetters (all right, perhaps not), the appearance of André 3000 and Big Boi at award shows are always something to see. In this photo, the guys are shown at the 28th Annual American Music Awards.

4

The Takeover

By the time the group was ready to release a fourth album, everyone was buzzing about OutKast. The pressure was on as the world asked if the rap duo's popularity would survive the turn of the century.

To represent the group's ever-changing style, Dré switched his stage name to André 3000 before the release of the album. On October 31, 2000, OutKast hit the music world with one of the most creative and critically acclaimed projects in hip-hop: *Stankonia*. The energetic album debuted at #2 on the charts and went triple platinum within a few months.

The three million people who bought a copy of the album were not disappointed. *Stankonia* saw the development of the perfect balance between the styles of Big Boi and André 3000. Displaying OutKast's diverse musical influences, the album combined classic funk beats with rock and hip-hop elements. "B.O.B." was a popular single, and the album as a whole received excellent reviews. In February 2001, "Ms. Jackson" became their first #1 pop single. The song was an apology to the mother of a girl-friend who had a baby, declaring that the father would still support his child even though he did not want to continue a romantic relationship with the young mother. The lyrics were more honest and heartfelt than most hip-hop songs, and a tight background track kept listeners interested.

OutKast's mind-blowing creativity did not go unnoticed. They were nominated for five awards at the 44th Annual Grammy Awards, held on February 27, 2002, and they won the honors for Best Rap Performance by a Duo or Group for "Ms. Jackson" and Best Rap Album for *Stankonia*. OutKast had officially arrived at the top.

Presenting ◆◆◆

OutKast had now achieved enough success during their careers to release an album of their greatest hits. Big Boi and Dré Present . . . OutKast hit stores on December 4, 2001. The album consisted of sixteen tracks, with hits such as "Rosa Parks" and "Ms. Jackson," as well as three new songs. One of the new tracks on the album was "The Whole World," featuring Killer Mike. In 2003, that song earned OutKast the Grammy for Best Rap Performance by a Duo or Group. "The Whole World" discussed the confusing political and emotional backdrop of the early twenty-first century, and audiences paid attention as the duo proved once again that rappers could be intelligent and socially conscious.

In addition to their own albums, OutKast could be heard on various compilations. The soundtracks for the popular films *Any Given Sunday* and *8 Mile* featured OutKast songs. It was appropriate that the rap duo would musically contribute to movies about football and the ghetto, respectively, because those themes shaped their youth. Other musical artists clearly recognized the duo's brilliance, and some even directly included OutKast songs in their own music. For example, Macy

Speakerboxxx/The Love Below was as unique as the artists them-selves. Big Boi's *Speakerboxxx* emphasized catchy rhythms and rap. Of course the fact that the guys had separate albums fueled rumors that the group was breaking up.

Gray's single "Do Something" uses a **sample** of the hit "Git Up, Git Out." Audiences and fellow musicians alike appreciated the incredible uniqueness of OutKast's sound.

Hitting the Charts Twice as Hard

However, the best was yet to come. Although their stylistic and visionary blend had characterized their previous albums, the duo decided to release a dual album so they could each explore a sound that was completely their own. They still performed as OutKast, but André 3000 and Big Boi created essentially independent projects. Big Boi explored catchy beats and rap techniques on what became *Speakerboxxx*, while André listened to punk bands to inspire a melody-driven album called *The Love Below*. André described the creative process of the album to VH1:

> *"The Love Below started out as a solo project, but every time I did a song, I came to the studio and I'm like, 'Check this out. What do you think?' Big Boi would be like, 'That's jamming, man!' When Big Boi would record a song, he would be like, 'Check this out!' I would be like, 'That's jamming!' It was almost like being a fan of OutKast and being in the group, I'm hearing songs like for the first time, so I'm like a fan of OutKast! Like, . . . wheee!"*

On September 23, 2003, OutKast released their career-defining double album, *Speakerboxxx/The Love Below*. The album debuted at #1 on the charts and sold over four million copies in just a few months. "Hey Ya!" and "The Way You Move" held *Billboard*'s #1 and #2 spots, respectively, for over two months. This beat the Bee Gees' 1978 record of a single group keeping both top spots for four weeks with "Night Fever" and "Stayin' Alive." OutKast was truly making music history.

OutKast enjoyed the most popular success with the peppy song "Hey Ya!" from *The Love Below*. André started creating "Hey Ya!" in 1999, and the working title was "Thank God for Mom and Dad." The song discusses the state of relationships today, because André observed that many couples stay together out of tradition instead of breaking up and seeking happiness elsewhere. Even though it had a serious subject matter, the entire package was so catchy and upbeat that it was considered more of a dance tune than a comment on modern society. The song was recorded in two days, and André played all of the instruments except bass, which was played by Aaron Mills. Many of the exclamations and lyrics were impromptu, meaning that André did not plan what he was going to sing but just said it during the recording. One of the most famous lines from the song, "Shake it like a Polaroid picture," was the result of such improvisation.

The music video for "Hey Ya!" shows the television performance of an eccentric band in which André 3000 plays all the performers. In developing the idea for the video, André told VH1, "It was like, if I created my own band, what would it look like?" The instrumentalists and singers were given names and individual personalities, and André improvised different gestures for each character. The roles were inspired by André's alter egos, such as the video's hero "Ice Cold." André describes Ice Cold as "straightforward and brutally honest" and admits that he is based on André's darker side. "[Ice Cold] came about because I would say certain things about girls," he explained, "and my homeboys would be like, 'Oh, man, you ice cold for saying that!'"

While André was enjoying massive success with "Hey Ya!" Big Boi was watching his own hit, "The Way You Move" featuring Sleepy Brown, climb up the charts. Whereas André focused more on singing on The Love Below, Big Boi mainly rapped on *Speakerboxxx*. "The Way You Move" is more traditional hip-hop than André's single, and it discusses the way females carry themselves. As Big Boi told VH1, "The video is basically about the sensuality and beauty of a woman." In the video, Big Boi and his friends watch gorgeous women in a car garage, ritzy dance hall, and a safari setting.

André 3000's *The Love Below* spun off one of OutKast's biggest hits, "Hey Ya!" Many people were so caught up in the catchy tune that they didn't realize it was about a very serious subject.

The duo's popular success was reflected by critical honors. In 2004, OutKast received the desirable Album of the Year Grammy for *Speakerboxxx/The Love Below*. They also won Best Urban/Alternative Performance for "Hey Ya!" and Best Rap Album. Their other nominations included Producer of the Year, Non-Classical; Best Short Form Music Video for "Hey Ya!"; and Record of the Year for "Hey Ya!" They had shown the world that, although they could make amazing music together, both André 3000 and Big Boi were capable of standing alone.

Going Wild

Even though OutKast enjoyed the popularity of Speakerboxx/The Love Below, it was nearly impossible to create a follow-up that would meet everyone's expectations. Once an artist wins the Grammy for Album of the Year, it seems as though the only place they could possibly go is down. Instead of trying to imitate the methods that had worked on their previous albums, OutKast took a risk and started to create something completely different than anything seen or heard in hip-hop: they decided to create a retro musical film featuring original OutKast music.

Idlewild is a musical drama about a 1930s Southern speakeasy. The R-rated film explores the lives of Percival (played by André), the club's shy piano player, and Rooster (Big Boi), the showy lead performer and manager. The two men are very different and have separate struggles, but they share a love of music. OutKast wrote original songs for the film, but the duo insisted that it would be different from a typical musical in that the characters sing in the club instead of randomly bursting out into song. Idlewild combined drama, music, cinema, and style. It was the feature film directing debut for Bryan Barber, who had collaborated with OutKast for numerous music videos. Three-time Tony Award winner Hinton Battle

Speakerboxxx/The Love Below was not ignored at award time. It won many and was nominated for many more. The album set also proved that André 3000 and Big Boi were not dependent on each other for success.

created the complex dance numbers. The film was released in U.S. theaters on August 25, 2006, to modest success.

Overall, the music of the film was more popular than the movie itself. The *Idlewild* soundtrack was released on August 22, 2006, and was soon certified platinum. At the Grammy Awards in 2007, OutKast was nominated for Best Urban/Alternative Performance for "Idlewild Blue (Don't Chu Worry 'Bout Me)" and Best Rap Performance by a Duo or Group for "Mighty 'O.'" Although they did not win in either of these categories, the honor of being considered proved to them and everyone else that their bold move had not failed.

Real life often plays a role in OutKast songs. André 3000 has a son with singer Erykah Badu, and he says that the way he treated her was not unlike the way Ice Cold treated women.

Beyond Rap

"You have to use this as your diving board almost," Big Boi said about a career in the music industry to VH1.

"You can say, 'I'm gonna rap and make records forever,' but just know that at some point, you're not gonna be the man no more. So before you get to that point, be the man in other things—real estate, municipal bonds, the stock market."

While OutKast is not taking on such projects as real estate and municipal bonds, they certainly explore other areas besides rap. Whether taking care of their children, working solo, landing movie roles, creating a cartoon series, or designing clothes, André and Big Boi keep themselves very busy.

Baby Mama Drama

Critics have praised OutKast for their meaningful, personal lyrics. André and Big Boi usually write about their real experiences, so their music offers a glimpse into their lives. The hit single "Ms. Jackson," for example, is from the perspective of an unwed father as he apologizes to his baby mama's mother for not marrying her daughter.

Both André and Big Boi have faced this difficult situation. André has a son named Seven Sirius with R&B artist Erykah Badu, who is featured on the powerful song "Liberation" from *Aquemini*. Although André once considered Erykah his soul mate, they ended their relationship shortly after Seven was born in 1997. André admits that he had treated Erykah in the same harsh manner that his "Hey Ya!" alter ego Ice Cold treats women. He also recognizes that he has often put his career ahead of his son. He told Alicia Quarles of the Associate Press,

> *"I'm not married or anything. I'm not as responsible as I should be. . . . A lot of times, weekends or holidays, certain days during the month, I get to see my kid. With his mom being an entertainer and me being an entertainer, I have to keep my life going to be able to support myself and him, it's kind of hard."*

Big Boi is not married but he also has kids: Jordan, Bamboo, and Cross. He is closer to his kids than André is to his son, and Big Boi occasionally brings them to the studio. He also enjoys going to amusement parks and playing football with them. He says he hopes his children will be happy and independent and that they will follow their own passions instead of trying to live up to the expectations of other people. They should not feel forced to be musicians or to follow in their father's footsteps, Big Boi says, because he would rather see his children happy than wealthy.

Each in their own way, both André and Big Boi have done the best they can as fathers. But both continue to struggle to balance their busy careers with fatherhood.

Solo, But Not So Long

In addition to having different musical styles, Big Boi and André have different personalities and interests. For example, André is a vegan, meaning that he does not consume any product that comes from an animal; Big Boi loves eating barbeque chicken. While André refuses drugs and alcohol, Big Boi's mansion has a wild party room called "The Boom Boom Room." It is only natural, therefore, that each member of the duo would like to explore various projects on his own. They proved to the world through Speakerboxxx/The Love Below that they could produce music independently of each other and still keep the originality that had defined their careers.

Rumors that OutKast is breaking up have followed the duo for years. The release of the dual album especially sparked speculation, although André and Big Boi denied that they planned to split. André's decision to not tour with Big Boi after the release of *Speakerboxxx/The Love Below* fanned the flames of gossip. "A lot of people don't understand that we've been doing it for like 11 years, professionally," André explained to VH1 in 2003. "You get to a point where you just want to be in the studio and the road is just not really appealing to me right now."

In music and in other areas, the members of OutKast have made it clear that they are each free to pursue their own dreams while still maintaining their friendship. André himself put it best when he said, "I mean, it's growing up, man. It ain't breaking up."

Big Names on the Big Screen

Besides the OutKast musical *Idlewild*, the duo has appeared in various other films. In March 2006, Big Boi played the adult Marcus in ATL, a film about four teens in working-class Atlanta who release their energy through roller skating and hip-hop. In July 2007, he also appeared in the golf comedy *Who's You Caddy?* with Faizon Love.

André has been even more involved in films. He has been interested in acting since performing in the play *Charlotte's Web* as a child, and he considers his musical performances a form of acting. He has been in character since he started his music career, because the zany behavior of André 3000 is separate from André's true, timid nature. Working in films seemed natural to him as a result, and after the release of *Speakerboxxx/The Love Below*, he moved from Atlanta to Los Angeles to pursue an acting career. He played a screenwriter alongside Harrison Ford in *Hollywood Homicide* in 2003 and was a musical prodigy named Valentine in 2004's *Love Hater*, directed by Morgan Freeman. That same year, André began shooting *Be Cool*, the sequel to *Get Shorty*, playing a member of the fictional rap group the Dub MDs. The 2005 release showed that André had a gift for comedy as he played the humorous gangster wannabe. Taking on a more serious role, André played family man Jeremiah in John Singleton's 2005 revenge film, *Four Brothers*. He was considered to play Jimi Hendrix in a Hughes Brothers biopic, but the filming of this production has encountered delays. He also explored television acting, appearing on a 2004 episode of the f/x drama *The Shield*. In November 2006, he took on a new role as the star and executive producer of the animated series *Class of 3000* on Cartoon Network. He voices Sunny Bridges, a recording superstar who abandons his fame so that he can teach and guide a class of musical prodigies at an Atlanta performing-arts school. André writes original songs for the show, making it a hit with young fans. Clearly, André's talents extend beyond the musical sphere.

Dress for Success

OutKast has received nearly as much attention for their unique fashion choices as for their music. In 2001, Big Boi founded the OutKast clothing line for men. However, the duo did not have as much control over the designs as they desired, and André created his own André Benjamin line of clothing and accessories in 2004. The line was featured in the "Hey Ya!" music video. André describes the clothes as "casual, individual, identity wear." In September 2004, *Esquire* magazine named André the world's best-dressed man. The rapper, who was known for his stylistic individuality throughout his career, says he draws inspiration for his outfits from period films and from the clothes of elderly men in his neighborhood. His fashion icons are Ralph Lauren, Sly Stone, and Jacqueline

Though both men have created clothing lines, André 3000's has been the most successful. In 2004, Esquire magazine named him the best-dressed man in the world. At last his sense of style was appreciated.

Kennedy. As he remarked to *Esquire*, fashion is more about self-confidence than about fitting in. "To me, that's real style, anything that feels comfortable and expresses your personality and makes you stand a little taller." Although some people have criticized André for his bizarre outfits, he is certainly an individual!

The Legends

"A rapper's lifespan can be short, but it can also be legendary," Big Boi commented to VH1.

"You can go on tour for years and years, if you got that dope stage show and spent your time in the studio giving these people quality albums instead of two or three songs and the rest crap."

Since they have achieved such an impressive level of success, OutKast has started trying to help emerging artists follow their dreams. The duo used to run Aquemini Records, but André distanced himself from the label so that he could pursue his acting interests. The first artist OutKast signed to its label was Slimm Calhoun. When André left, Big Boi took over and renamed the company the Purple Ribbon Label, which is distributed by Virgin Records. The name refers to a high quality of canines in the dog-breeding world: when a dog is purple-ribbon-bred and its pedigree is purple, you can count three generations of the dog. This is an appropriate title, because Big Boi has bred and sold pit bulls to celebrities such as Serena Williams and Usher since 2001 through his own Pitfall Kennels. He expanded the label to create Purple Ribbon Films, of which he is the CEO. Purple Ribbon has helped many artists find their way in the music industry. Big Boi has also started producing records; his production crews are called Beat Bullies and Boom Boom Room Productions.

While Big Boi helps new artists find their footing, André is giving a new meaning to the term "music artist." He not only raps, but he plays numerous instruments and hopes to learn more. He regularly practices clarinet and saxophone, and he hopes to attend the high-status Julliard School of Music to study classical music composition and theory. He amazes audiences visually as well; he loves to paint, and his artwork can be purchased through his Sevenaire Paintings venture.

In any field, OutKast continues to be one of the most innovative and intriguing groups in the mainstream. "We started straight from the street level, underground," Big Boi told VH1.

"We were like SARS almost. It was contagious and it caught on. For us, it's all about the music. We make music for everybody to hear, and you can dig what we're talking about, you can come on and get down with us. If not, keep it moving. It's not our fault. Blame the music. It reaches out and touches that many people, because people can relate to what we're talking about."

Although their sound is difficult to define, their effect on audiences everywhere can be described with one simple word: incredible!

1970s Hip-hop is born in the New York City borough of the Bronx.

Feb. 1, 1975 Antwan André Patton, Big Boi, is born.

May 27, 1975 André Lauren Benjamin, André 3000, is born.

1994 "Player's Ball" becomes OutKast's first #1 single.

1994 *Southernplayalisticadillacmuzik*, their first album, is released.

1995 OutKast is named Best New Rap Group at the Source Awards.

1996 *ATLiens* is released.

1998 *Aquemini* is released.

1999 OutKast receives its first Grammy nomination for "Rosa Parks."

1999 Rosa Parks files a lawsuit against OutKast and the record label over the song "Rosa Parks"; the case is dismissed.

2000 *Stankonia* is released.

2001 OutKast wins its first Grammy Awards.

2001 "Ms. Jackson" becomes the group's first #1 pop single.

2001 *Big Boi and Dré Present . . . OutKast,* a greatest hits album, is released.

2002 OutKast wins another Grammy Award.

2003 OutKast wins three Grammy Awards.

2003 The lawsuit between Rosa Parks and OutKast is reinstated.

2003 *Speakerboxxx/The Love Below* is released, debuting at #1.

2005 The lawsuit between Rosa Parks and OutKast is settled, with no admission of guilt.

2006 OutKast's film *Idlewild* debuts.

Albums

1994	*Southernplayalisticadillacmuzik*
1996	*ATLiens*
1998	*Aquemini*
2000	*Stankonia*
2001	*Big Boi and Dre Present . . . OutKast*
2003	*Seakerboxxx/The Love Below*
2006	*Idlewild*

Number-One Singles

1994	"Player's Ball"
1996	"Elevators (Me & You)"
2000	"Ms. Jackson"
2003	"Hey Ya!"
2003	"The Way You Move"

DVDs

2001	*Uncovered*
2003	*OutKast—The Videos*
2003	*The Way You Move/Hey Ya!*

2004   *Psychedelic Funk Soul Brothers*

2005   *Dare to Be Different*

Film

2006   *Idlewild*

Awards/Recognition

1995   Source Award: Best New Rap Group.

2001   Grammy Award: Best Rap Performance by a Duo or Group ("Ms. Jackson"), Best Rap Album (*Stankonia*); MTV Video Music Award: Best Hip-Hop Video ("Ms. Jackson").

2002   Grammy Award: Best Rap Performance by a Duo or Group ("The Whole World," with Killer Mike).

2003   Grammy Award: Album of the Year (*Speakerboxxx/The Love Below*), Best Urban/Alternative Performance ("Hey Ya!"), Best Rap Album (*Speakerboxxx/The Love Below*).

Books

Bogdanov, Vladimir, Chris Woodstra, Steven Thomas Erlewine, and John Bush (eds.). *All Music Guide to Hip-Hop: The Definitive Guide to Rap and Hip-Hop*. San Francisco, Calif.: Backbeat Books, 2003.

Chang, Jeff. *Can't Stop Won't Stop: A History of the Hip-Hop Generation*. New York: Picador, 2005.

Emcee Escher and Alex Rappaport. *The Rapper's Handbook: A Guide to Freestyling, Writing Rhymes, and Battling*. New York: Flocabulary Press, 2006.

George, Nelson. *Hip Hop America*. New York: Penguin, 2005.

Kusek, Dave, and Gerd Leonhard. *The Future of Music: Manifesto for the Digital Music Revolution*. Boston, Mass.: Berkley Press, 2005.

Light, Alan (ed.). *The Vibe History of Hip Hop*. New York: Three Rivers Press, 1999.

Nickson, Chris. *Hey Ya!* New York: St. Martin's, 2004.

Sarig, Roni, and Julia Beverly. *Third Coast: OutKast, Timbaland, and How Hip-Hop Became a Southern Thing*. New York: De Capo Press, 2007.

Waters, Rosa. *Hip-Hop: A Short History*. Broomall, Pa.: Mason Crest, 2007.

Watkins, S. Craig. *Hip Hop Matters: Politics, Pop Culture, and the Struggle for the Soul of a Movement*. Boston, Mass.: Beacon Press, 2006.

Web Sites

OutKast—Official Site
www.outkast.com

OutKast on MTV
www.mtv.com/music/outkast/artist.jhtml

OutKast on MySpace
www.myspace.com/outkast

OutKast on VH1
www.vh1.com/artists/az/outkast/artist.jhtml

Glossary

collaboration—The act of working with someone to produce something.

culture—The beliefs, customs, practices, and social behavior of a particular nation or people.

diverse—Different from each other.

ethnicities—Affiliations or distinctions based on shared cultural traits.

freestyle—Done without preparation.

funk—A musical style that is based on jazz, blues, and soul and that is characterized by a heavy rhythmic bass and backbeat.

genre—A category into which an artwork can be placed based on its subject, media, or style.

mainstream—The ideas, actions, and values that are most widely accepted by a group or society.

platinum—A designation indicating that a recording has sold one million units.

R&B—Rhythm and blues; a style of music that combines elements of blues and jazz, and that was originally developed by African American musicians.

remix—A re-recording of a piece of music.

sample—A portion of a previously recorded piece of music used in another recording.

scratching—Purposely dragging the record needle across a spinning record.

tracks—Separate pieces of music on a disk, tape, or record.

Index

About the Author

Jacquelyn Simone is continuing her education in upstate New York, where she is pursuing a degree in journalism. She has always been fascinated by different musical genres and enjoys singing and playing guitar as well as listening to music.

Picture Credits

istockphoto.com: p. 16
  London, Cat: p. 22
PR Photos: pp. 11, 31, 32
  Bielawski, Adam: p. 46
  Gabber, David: p. 44
  Harris, Glenn: p. 51
  Hatcher, Chris: p. 8
  Mayer, Janet: p. 42
  Mejia, Ed: pp. 28, 39
  Thompson, Terry: front cover, pp. 2, 12, 24, 36
  Wild1: p. 21

To the best knowledge of the publisher, all other images are in the public domain. If any image has been inadvertently uncredited, please notify Harding House Publishing Service, Vestal, New York 13850, so that rectification can be made for future printings.